ABUNDANT TRUTH INTERNATIONAL MINISTRIES

Kingdom Discipleship Series

Keys to Service

Mastering the Art of Christian Servanthood

Roderick Levi Evans

Published by Abundant Truth Publishing
P.O. Box 126 * Camden, NC 27921
Phone: 1-877-841-7209 * Fax: 1-877-841-7209
Web: www.abundantpublishing.net
Email: abundantpublishing@gmail.com

Printed U.S.A.

Front & Back Cover Designs by Abundant Truth Publishing
Image by Gerd Altmann from Pixabay

> Abundant Truth Publishing is a ministry of Abundant Truth International Ministries. The primary mission of ATI Ministries is to equip the Body of Christ with tools necessary to defend and contend for the truth of the Christian faith. Jesus Christ came to bear witness of the truth and ATI Ministries is a modern-day extension of His commission (John 18:37).

Keys to Service: Mastering the Art of Christian Servanthood
©2024 Abundant Truth Publishing
All Rights Reserved

ISBN: 978-1-60141-613-1

Unless otherwise indicated, all of the scripture quotations are taken from the *Authorized King James Version* of the Bible. Scripture quotations marked with NIV are taken from the *New International Version* of the Bible. Scripture quotations marked with NASV are taken from the *New American Standard Version* of the Bible. Scripture quotations marked with Amplified are taken from the *Amplified Bible*.

Contents

Introduction

Chapter 1 - Mastering the Art of Servanthood   1

The Goal of Servanthood   5

The Drive of Servanthood   6

Chapter 2 - Lessons from Paul's Conversion   11

Allow Others to Serve   16

Allow Humility in Service   17

Allow Servanthood Position   19

Allow God's Direction   20

Allow Forgiveness   22

Contents *(cont.)*

Chapter 3 - Challenges to Servanthood	27
Perception of Self	31
Perspective of God	33
Scripture Text: Acts 9:1-19	39
Bibliography	45

Introduction

Jesus called His followers disciples. A **disciple** is a convinced adherent of a school or individual who accepts and assists in spreading the doctrines of another. A Christian must not only believe on Jesus but be willing to share the faith of Jesus Christ. In order to do this, the believer has to not only understand his role as a disciple but know how to defend his beliefs.

The Kingdom Discipleship Series explores the biblical truths that should assist the believer in developing as a disciple of Christ. Not only will Christians grow in their walk with the Lord, but their understanding of foundational biblical truths will also expand.

In this issue

Service is a vital aspect of the Christian walk and experience. Each member of the Body of Christ is called to serve others. Jesus claimed that He did not come to be served, but to serve. This should be the attitude of every Christian.

In this publication, we will discuss the Christian call to servanthood. Though obstacles and challenges exist, Christian can master the art of servitude. Be encouraged to know that fruitful Chrisian service is attainable.

KEYS TO SERVICE

-Chapter 1-

Mastering the Art of Servanthood

KEYS TO SERVICE

Kingdom Discipleship Series 2

KEYS TO SERVICE

In mastering the art of servanthood, we have to know how to serve others which comes with difficulties. These difficulties are enhanced when those whom we serve may not seem as if they need, want, desire, or deserve our service.

KEYS TO SERVICE

Kingdom Discipleship Series

KEYS TO SERVICE

Jesus told the disciples that the one who wanted to be great would have to be the one who served.

The Goal of Servanthood

Having a mindset of service and servanthood is necessary for fruitful ministry, whatever it may be. Without having a mind to serve, you become an unprofitable servant and disciple.

However, we know that those who serve faithfully in the Kingdom of God can look forward to the day when God

KEYS TO SERVICE

says, "Well, done thou good and faithful servant." Hence, mastering the art of servanthood is crucial to success.

The Drive of Servanthood

What does it mean to serve? To serve is to be of use, to discharge a duty or function, to furnish or supply with something needed or desired; to comply with the commands or demands of.

Simply put, we must remain useful to Christ and serve at His command and not according to our desires.

KEYS TO SERVICE

We can desire to serve, but we must serve in the area that Christ has purposed for us. Else, we can serve out of place and become a hindrance rather than help. We must serve according to His will and with the proper character.

This is where the challenge to serve becomes difficult. How? It is because our service will always directly impact, influence, and involve others.

In mastering the art of servant-

KEYS TO SERVICE

hood, we have to know how to serve others which comes with difficulties. These difficulties are enhanced when those whom we serve may not seem as if they need, want, desire, or deserve our service.

KEYS TO SERVICE

Personal Thoughts:

_____

_____

_____

_____

_____

_____

_____

KEYS TO SERVICE

KEYS TO SERVICE

-Chapter 2-

Lessons from Paul's Conversion

KEYS TO SERVICE

KEYS TO SERVICE

And there was a certain disciple at Damascus, named Ananias; and to him said the Lord in a vision, Ananias. And he said, Behold, I am here, Lord. Acts 9:10 (KJV)

KEYS TO SERVICE

KEYS TO SERVICE

In recalling the account of Paul's conversion, we discover a disciple by the name of Ananias who Christ challenged to be of service to Paul, who was known for his hatred of the Church.

It had to be difficult for Ananias to be of service to a man who seemed not to want, need, or deserve it.

However, he rose to the occasion and rendered service to Saul (Paul), who would be one of the greatest proponents of the Christian faith. We

KEYS TO SERVICE

can learn 6 dynamics (from Saul and Ananias) of the art of servanthood from this story. Please read Acts chapter 9:1-19 (included at the end of the book) for the full account.

Allow Others to Serve

From Saul (Paul), we learn that you must allow others to serve or your service can be destructive, even against Christ *(Read Acts 9:1-5)*.

Saul (Paul) was rendering a service in the name of God while frustrating the work of God (through persecuting the Christians).

As we serve, we must not destroy others who are trying to render service to Christ even when we do not agree with their method or manner.

Make sure you allow others to serve in conjunction with your service because they are members of His Body.

Allow Humility in Service

From Saul, we learn that you have to be humble to God and let Him direct you as to how you serve.

KEYS TO SERVICE

And he trembling and astonished said, Lord, what wilt thou have me to do? And the Lord said unto him, Arise, and go into the city, and it shall be told thee what thou must do. Acts 9:6 (KJV)

After Christ revealed Himself to Saul, he had to wait for God, to let me know how He wanted him to serve. The same applies to the Christian today. You should not serve without a commission.

In order to serve properly, you

KEYS TO SERVICE

need to know what you should be doing. Guidance from leaders and others, accompanied with the inspiration of the Spirit makes this possible.

Allow Servanthood Position

Ananias placed himself in a position to serve by his personal walk with Christ.

And there was a certain disciple at Damascus, named Ananias; and to him said the Lord in a vision, Ananias. And

KEYS TO SERVICE

he said, Behold, I am here, Lord. Acts 9:10 (KJV)

When we turn our attention to Ananias, we see an important truth. He was in prayer. This is the perfect position to receive clear direction for how he was to serve. If you want to serve effectively and assuredly spend time seeking Christ and service will follow.

Allow God's Direction

Ananias received specific instructions. He was sure to follow

KEYS TO SERVICE

them.

> *And the Lord said unto him, Arise, and go into the street which is called Straight, and enquire in the house of Judas for one called Saul, of Tarsus: for, behold, he prayeth, And hath seen in a vision a man named Ananias coming in, and putting his hand on him, that he might receive his sight. Acts 9:11-12 (KJV)*

When you are given the charge to serve, make sure you receive

KEYS TO SERVICE

instructions for your service – from God and the leadership that places you (if that is the case). Never be a loose cannon in the kingdom of God. *Your service is needed, but it needs direction.*

Allow Forgiveness

Ananias had to get over what he knew about Saul.

Then Ananias answered, Lord, I have heard by many of this man, how much evil he hath done to thy saints at Jerusalem: And here he

KEYS TO SERVICE

hath authority from the chief priests to bind all that call on thy name. Acts 9:13-14 (KJV)

Do not allow what you know about people, what you have experienced by the hands of people, or a person's disposition stop you from being willing and obedient to render service to them. Without this mindset, your service will be frustrated and unfruitful.

KEYS TO SERVICE

KEYS TO SERVICE

Personal Thoughts:

_____

_____

_____

_____

_____

_____

_____

_____

KEYS TO SERVICE

KEYS TO SERVICE

-Chapter 3-

Challenges to Servanthood

KEYS TO SERVICE

KEYS TO SERVICE

But the Lord said unto him, Go thy way: for he is a chosen vessel unto me, to bear my name before the Gentiles, and kings, and the children of Israel: For I will shew him how great things he must suffer for my name's sake. Acts 9:15-16 (KJV)

KEYS TO SERVICE

KEYS TO SERVICE

Challenges to servanthood are difficult to overcome and cannot be avoided. However, many of the difficulties are internal.

One must face one's personal perceptions and one's trust in God's faithfulness. From the account of Ananias and Saul, we discover two main truths that can be the basis for faithfulness in servanthood.

Perception of Self

Get over your personal obstacles and obey the Lord.

KEYS TO SERVICE

But the Lord said unto him, Go thy way: for he is a chosen vessel unto me, to bear my name before the Gentiles, and kings, and the children of Israel: For I will shew him how great things he must suffer for my name's sake. Acts 9:15-16 (KJV)

Ananias had to get over his personal problems with Saul to serve.

As Christians, many internal and external obstacles will present themselves to deter us from service. Obstacles can cause apprehensions to pursue service. Though apprehensions may exist, we have to overcome them and serve faithfully.

Perspective of God

God proved Ananias' service as Saul was healed and strengthened.

And Ananias went his way and entered into the house; and putting his hands on him said, Brother Saul, the Lord, even Jesus, that appeared unto thee in the

KEYS TO SERVICE

way as thou camest, hath sent me, that thou mightest receive thy sight, and be filled with the Holy Ghost. And immediately there fell from his eyes as it had been scales: and he received sight forthwith, and arose, and was baptized. And when he had received meat, he was strengthened. Then was Saul certain days with the disciples which were at Damascus. Acts 9:17-19 (KJV)

When you have a mind to serve,

KEYS TO SERVICE

you can expect Christ to be with you and show His presence, power, and peace in you. Ananias saw the results of his service and you will too. Go on to master the art of servanthood.

God will always be faithful to those whom He gives a commission. Internal and external obstacles will surface. It is a fact!

However, one must remember the faithfulness of God. Many numerous biblical accounts attest to God's faithfulness.

KEYS TO SERVICE

You can overcome and have the testimony that God enables us to be able to master the art of servanthood.

KEYS TO SERVICE

Personal Thoughts:

_____

_____

_____

_____

_____

_____

_____

_____

_____

KEYS TO SERVICE

KEYS TO SERVICE

Scripture Text:

Acts 9:1-19

1 And Saul, yet breathing out threatenings and slaughter against the disciples of the Lord, went unto the high priest,

2 And desired of him letters to Damascus to the synagogues, that if he found any of this way, whether they were men or women, he might bring them bound unto Jerusalem.

3 And as he journeyed, he came near

KEYS TO SERVICE

Damascus: and suddenly there shined round about him a light from heaven:

4 And he fell to the earth, and heard a voice saying unto him, Saul, Saul, why persecutest thou me?

5 And he said, Who art thou, Lord? And the Lord said, I am Jesus whom thou persecutest:

it is hard for thee to kick against the pricks.

6 And he trembling and astonished said, Lord, what wilt thou have me to do? And the Lord said unto him, Arise, and go

into the city, and it shall be told thee what thou must do.

7 And the men which journeyed with him stood speechless, hearing a voice, but seeing no man.

8 And Saul arose from the earth; and when his eyes were opened, he saw no man: but they led him by the hand, and brought him into Damascus.

9 And he was three days without sight, and neither did eat nor drink.

10 And there was a certain disciple at Damascus, named Ananias; and to him

KEYS TO SERVICE

said the Lord in a vision, Ananias. And he said, Behold, I am here, Lord.

11 And the Lord said unto him, Arise, and go into the street which is called Straight, and enquire in the house of Judas for one called Saul, of Tarsus: for, behold, he prayeth,

12 And hath seen in a vision a man named Ananias coming in, and putting his hand on him, that he might receive his sight.

13 Then Ananias answered, Lord, I have heard by many of this man, how much

evil he hath done to thy saints at Jerusalem:

14 And here he hath authority from the chief priests to bind all that call on thy name.

15 But the Lord said unto him, Go thy way: for he is a chosen vessel unto me, to bear my name before the Gentiles, and kings, and the children of Israel:

16 For I will shew him how great things he must suffer for my name's sake.

17 And Ananias went his way, and entered into the house; and putting his

hands on him said, Brother Saul, the Lord, even Jesus, that appeared unto thee in the way as thou camest, hath sent me, that thou mightest receive thy sight, and be filled with the Holy Ghost.

18 And immediately there fell from his eyes as it had been scales: and he received sight forthwith, and arose, and was baptized.

19 And when he had received meat, he was strengthened. Then was Saul certain days with the disciples which were at Damascus.

Bibliography

Smith, William. *Smith's Bible Dictionary.* Holman Bible Publishers. Nashville, Tennessee. c1994

The Bible Library. *The Bible Library CD Rom Disc.* Ellis Enterprises Incorporated, (c)1988 – 2000. 4205 McAuley Blvd., Suite 385, Oklahoma City, OK 73120. All Rights Reserved.

KEYS TO SERVICE

Lockman Foundation. *Comparative Study Bible.* Zondervan Publishing House. Grand Rapids, MI, c1984

KEYS TO SERVICE

Study Notes:

KEYS TO SERVICE

KEYS TO SERVICE

KEYS TO SERVICE

KEYS TO SERVICE

KEYS TO SERVICE

KEYS TO SERVICE

KEYS TO SERVICE

KEYS TO SERVICE

KEYS TO SERVICE

KEYS TO SERVICE

KEYS TO SERVICE

KEYS TO SERVICE

KEYS TO SERVICE

KEYS TO SERVICE

KEYS TO SERVICE

KEYS TO SERVICE

KEYS TO SERVICE

www.ingramcontent.com/pod-product-compliance
Lightning Source LLC
Chambersburg PA
CBHW050344010526
44119CB00049B/689